Virgin Territory

OTHER BOOKS BY BETSY STRUTHERS:

Poetry:

Censored Letters. Mosaic Press, 1984
Saying So Out Loud. Mosaic Press, 1988
Running Out Of Time. Wolsak and Wynn, 1993

Fiction:

Found: A Body. Simon & Pierre, 1992
Grave Deeds. Simon & Pierre, 1994
A Studied Death. Simon & Pierre, 1995

Non-Fiction:

Poets in the Classroom, co-edited with Sarah Klassen. Pembroke Press, 1995

Virgin Territory

Betsy Struthers

Wolsak and Wynn . Toronto

Copyright © Betsy Struthers 1996

All rights reserved. No part of this book may be reproduced or transmitted in any form, by any means, electronic or mechanical, without permission in writing from the publisher, except by a reviewer who may quote brief passages in a review.

Typeset in Times Roman, printed in Canada by
The Coach House Printing Company, Toronto

Front cover art: *Kore* by Catherine McIntosh Jeffery
Cover design: C. McIntosh Jeffery, F. Treadwell and B. Struthers
Author's photo: Florence Treadwell

Some of these poems, or earlier versions of them, appeared in: *Arc, Canadian Literature, CV II, The Fiddlehead, The Malahat Review, The People's Poetry Newsletter,* and *Room of One's Own.* "Thin Ice" appeared in *That Sign of Perfection,* edited by John B. Lee (Black Moss Press, 1995).

For caring, and for thoughtful criticism, the author thanks Troon Harrison, Susan McMaster, Florence Treadwell, Christl Verduyn, and Richard Harrison; and in all ways Ned Struthers and Jim Struthers.

The author also thanks thanks the Canada Council for the Arts Grant B which funded time in which to write these poems, and to the Ontario Arts Council for Writers Reserve grants.

The publishers gratefully acknowledge support from The Canada Council and The Ontario Arts Council which has made publication of this book possible.

Wolsak and Wynn Publishers Ltd.
Don Mills Post Office Box 316
Don Mills, Ontario, Canada, M3C 2S7

Canadian Cataloguing in Publication Data

Struthers, Betsy, 1951-
  Virgin Territory
Poems.
ISBN 0-919897-51-7
I. Title.
PS8587.T7298V56 1996   C811'.54   C96-931120-6
PR9199.3.S77V56 1996

for my sisters,
Susan Durrant and Catherine Porter

Contents

ENCOUNTERING THE CRONE

Of the flesh . . .

Sins of the mothers	11
Turned turtle	13
Out of the depths	15
A last supper	16
Confession	17
Crown-of-thorns	19
Vision	21
Encountering the crone	23

And of the spirit . . .

In translation	27
Degrees of ascension	28
Come down	29
Bred in the bone	30
Birds of passage	31
In the sanctuary	32
Acts of worship	34
Visitation on the beach	35
(Still	36
In sites made sacred	38
Confronting the source	40
Under the surface	41
The oracle speaks	42

COMING OF AGE

The mummy	47
Son underground	48
Country matters	50
Gone fishing	51
Siege of herons, murder of crows	52
Coming of age	53
Reunion	56
When friends divorce	57
Parting friends	58
Thin ice	62
The daughter element	64

VIRGIN TERRITORY

First time	71
Virgin territory	73
Evensong	75
Mouth to mouth	76
Speaking in tongues	77
Utter silence	78
The lure of the deep	79
Celebrating the solstice	82
Acts of communion	84
A kind of catechism	87

ENDNOTES   88

ENCOUNTERING THE CRONE

Of the flesh . . .

SINS OF THE MOTHERS

Here is a family in which the word *love*
is not said aloud, in which sisters
shake hands when they meet, when they part
they do not kiss. From generation
unto generation, the mothers
have tried to control us, they
forbid their daughters to marry,
they weep themselves into clinics
or will not speak to us for years,
our duty presents left on doorknobs,
our phone calls unanswered.

Here is a family full of heart disease,
mothers sinking down on sofas, hands
on their left breasts, mouths pinched
in an oh! of pained surprise. *How
can you do this to me?* repeats
mother after grandmother after
great-grandmother, the chain
of weddings barely borne,
each daughter weighted with
her mother's veil, tulle stained
by time and tears.

Still we have followed the desires
of our own hearts, one after the other we lie
in the beds we have made and are there
made joyful. And though we may
seek to cut off these apron strings,
when Grandma calls us back to her
small room, begs us to hold her one
more time as we have let her hold
on to us, we can't deny this kiss,
lips pursed as she turns
her cheek.

TURNED TURTLE

To command such stillness,
the apparent rest of skull on wrinkled neck,
hooded eyes that have seen all
they will see and now reflect
the whirl of years and years,
a kaleidoscope of red inside the lids,
chaos of blood made mute
by cataracts, the fall of light
through lowered blinds.

To be pried from the shell
of a home that has turned
against her, trapped her
all night in the tub,
she who hated to swim,
who came to the beach
in a flowered dress
to watch us splash,
minnows she called us,
catching us up, hugging us,
her arms thin even then.

Cast adrift, flesh
shrinks from her bones.
She clutches her elbows
in fingers scraped to claws
and picks small wounds,
piteous stigmata, proof
she still can bleed,
though she can't recall
her address
and even household words
forsake her.

OUT OF THE DEPTHS

When I first saw that black knob, gnarled and thick as my fist,
rear from the still water; when the dome of her shell
parted the current with painstaking slowness
as if the bottom mud itself was rising;
when her eyes turned on me and for one moment opened
blank and flat as the tally of her ages,

Grandmother plucked me away from the edge, her mottled hand
a claw on my wrist. *It's dangerous,* she said, *to go in too deep.
There's more than fish down there, more than weeds
to draw you under.* She took me in, pulled the blinds
and prayed, while out on the lake the loons went crazy,
their young gone underwater.

And now, so much later, when I take you by the hand
down to the beach where an orange moon rides the horizon,
waves rearing up to kiss it: she visits me again, relic
out of time. She is not what we expect but comes
so close we have to fall apart before her, silenced
by her slow deliberation, her end in sight, home
forever on her back.

A LAST SUPPER

We come upon her as we still do unawares
startled by how small she is, how bowed,
how barely the curled white hair hides
the bumps and ridges of her skull.
She may look up when we greet her,
she may remember our names,
she may raise one hand from the arm
of her easy chair, the fingers crooked talons
that rest for a moment in our palms
and fall to fold one on the other
in an attitude of prayer. We shift
from foot to foot, talk loudly to each other
to avoid the smacking of her lips,
the murmur as she confers
with the husband dead twelve years,
who is with her always as we are not.
Yet we insist that she come with us,
that she sit at our table,
we fill her glass with wine,
her plate with meat and bread.
She doesn't eat. She doesn't
say the grace. She simply waits,
endures the flowers, the candles,
the song we sing for her. At least
we do sing for her, bring
cake, her silver spoons,
sterling heavy in our hands.

CONFESSION

I am waiting for her
to die. When the phone
rings before breakfast
my eyes close for a moment,
my thick tongue stutters
the prayer I cannot admit
not aloud, not in the company
of my sisters. We buy her
chocolates and fancy biscuits
she devours by the box,
throned in her husband's
red naugahyde recliner,
the one thing she wanted
when her household
was divided.   On her birthday
we crowd her white room,
perch on the edge of the single
high bed, admire framed pictures
gathered here together:
grandchildren, great-grandchildren,
their names a litany we chorus
to cover up the doubt we hear
in the pause as she peers at each,
considers her responses.

Times enough she knows
what has brought her here
what has brought us here
with our foolish gifts,
our hands behind our backs
in fists she turns
her pale eyes from.
Still we come, kneel
before her, her hands
light on our faces,
we close our eyes, yes,
flesh of her flesh,
her thorns, her
manifold sins.

CROWN-OF-THORNS

In the end we want to be of use, not just to clutter her room
with things she has no name for, tape player, video machine, red
eyes watching her even at noon, even when she turns over in
bed to face the white wall. What if she confuses our names?
She knows what makes us hers: cheekbones, set of eyes, shape
of legs, the ankles she always was so proud of, weeps to see
encased in thick elastic hose. She won't go for walks, can't
walk, can't stand the wheelchair though she lowers herself
into it, allows us to push her from the car park to the hothouse
which steams in fields of snow, her favourite time and place.
For now, she is quiet, face lifted to the damp caress of flowered
air, eyes closed, mouth open to the earth's moist secrets. She
will know them even better soon enough, her fingers fret the
crocheted quilt wrapped around her lap to hold her in. We know
that these are her final days and we want to be of use, to ease
her passage to whatever she believes lies beyond:
                            her husband, impatient, taps
a leather-soled shoe, looks at his watch again while she falls
behind, bends to straighten a wayward seam, gloves clutched in
her hand, matching hat with its veil tipped over one eye. Wait
for me, she is always calling. She can hardly see him for the
mist filtering through trumpet vines, she's made dizzy by the
breath of lilies crowding the worn brick path. Before her,
spread-eagled on the dripping glass, an espaliered crown-of-
thorns, like the one she kept for years in her south window.

Could this be her window and her plant grown enormous as she herself has shrunk? Her head bows under the weight of this idea, her temples throb, pricked by blood-red blooms. She's had enough. She cries out to us in a loud voice, Why has he left me to face this all alone?

VISION

        1.
Never would have a bird in the house, bad luck
I always thought she meant, but now I know
it had everything to do with cages, the false
security of the dropcloth; the singing
to artificial light; the way

she perches in the lobby, waiting, head cocked
to the click of the closing door; the way she scolds
the canary, yellow fluff huddled on newspaper,
when she fumbles the catch open, and it will not fly.

All of us talk about going away, to England, France,
Rome, any Old Country where things are
as they have always been, rooted in their proper places.
She won't believe she can find for herself

the room at the end of the longest hall that we call her room.
She takes us there past rows of bolted doors, key
quivering in her outstretched hand, its chain
wrapped around her blue wrist fluttering.

2.
Pretend, as we will, that she has nothing to do with the way
we are together in the kitchen, washing dishes,
steam from the sink clouding our glasses
so that we must dry them again and again, inside and out.

All of us, mother and daughters, short-sighted, though she,
Grandmother, will never admit to needing lenses. Her pale eyes
on us see everything, shortened hems, smudged lipstick,
the sidelong looks when she forgets and speaks his name

the one she is always talking to whom we insist is not here,
is dead, has been dead such a long time. When she says
he is coming for her, she has to stay awake,
we shake our heads, we consult our watches, we call

our own husbands to tell them we're delayed a little while
till she settles into sleep, curled, so small in the single bed.
This faith in fact we must confess we share with her: that they
will wait for us in rooms they've gone before us to prepare,

rooms with candlelight, red wine in crystal cups. And in the nest
the duvet makes, this coming home: flesh cleaves to flesh,
tangled limbs a knot of solid bones, a cradle rocked
with joined and breaking breaths.

ENCOUNTERING THE CRONE

Maybe she is only one of a trio of old ladies
who now sit side by side on a lobby sofa
basking in a puddle of sun, eyes closed,
hands on the knobs of their canes, backs bent
under the hump of their histories.

Maybe we call her grandmother, first
mother of all of us who wait for her to wake,
for her to notice that we're waiting. Maybe
this time she will be the wise woman
we've come here to consult, the one
who has been this way before, who
can tell us how to live this long,
how to survive not dying.

In the reek of cloves and shrivelled fruit,
the body continues to look after itself,
to feed and eliminate, keep warm, sleep,
skin folding itself over brittle bones.
All the secrets of its organs and fevers
have been probed and charted. Maybe
we can face the visible process
of decay. Maybe we bite our own lips
raw, deny the aches in our breasts,
the strain of breathing.

Maybe we hope so much
it is almost a prayer. Maybe this time
she will open clear eyes and see us,
open her arms to hold us.
We dare not doubt aloud, dare not
relax our vigil. It may be true:
this time she will answer,
not echo, our questions:
Where am I? Who?

And of the spirit . . .

IN TRANSLATION

Don't forget. Write me, she insists, her voice a quaver on the line.

I twirl the coiled wire round my wrist, phone static in my ear,
and try to find the words to say good-bye yet one more time,
my husband waving from the boarding gate, son pulling
on my other arm. It's not so easy to let go, to leave her
on the edge between the surface of the life she knows
and the darkness that must come. She's always been afraid
of heights and caves, and foreign lands and foreign tongues.
What I do now she can't approve, wanting love to be for home,
the family I was born to, not the one I choose. I'm leaving
for one month, for her forever, her sentence running on and out.
Remember is her final word, her grip on my hand. She
is the story I will tell my son when the lights inside are low,
the plane climbing, wings radiant, turning to the dawn.

DEGREES OF ASCENSION

We are rising in spite of ourselves, in spite
of what our bodies know of earth. Our toes
curl, prehensile, seek roots to hang on to,
the soles of our feet pressed flat, calves
tense, thighs ready for the leap, the fall.
Willing ourselves still, not to let go,
we yawn over and over, jaws stretch
behind clasped palms, snap shut,
teeth clench as we swallow again
and again ears pop with such effort.
The ground lurches and slips out
from under us, we're airborne,
our eyes turn to glass
clouded by atmosphere,
so many held breaths.

COME DOWN

So soon put in our place
by signs whose mixed letters
we take to be language.

Houses slump in empty streets
so narrow, arms outstretched
touch shutters left and right

And there's too much light for the hour
our watches insist on.

A cathedral confronts us, spire and dome,
and people at last, women in black
flocked on its steps

Shake their shawled heads at your beard,
my bare arms, our pale son. They turn inside
to candles and incense

While our hands out beg meaning
our tongues cannot master.

BRED IN THE BONE

When we enter the cathedral, its heavy doors
close easily behind us, easily
nudge us into this hushed gloom

That whisper, that muffled sigh,
is someone standing almost on our heels,
the ghost who belongs here,
who we bring in with us

I can't help bowing my head,
the guidebook trembles in my hands,
the last letter from home
stuffed between its pages

It doesn't matter
what I read there, or ignore,
the runes beneath our feet,
the symbols etched in glass,
the effigy on its tomb so
skilfully composed

Flesh interprets
for itself
the clenched lips
the stone stare
the stillness only
bones can know

BIRDS OF PASSAGE[1]

The language of birds is not an illusion: listen,
cock crow summons us to light, we can't
sleep, roll over and into each other, a knocking
of bones, a greeting of flesh
made slick with heat,
the weight of down.

Even their names translate
into song: *Alouette* we sing
driving to the Camargue, where nothing
is what we expect of France: savannas
of reeds part as we flush wild
horses, horned cows, and in the lagoons
flamingoes, long necks twined,
a sign our own bodies interpret
coupling hands.

Clouds mass black, shroud the horizon
in streaks of light racked by thunder.
Car lashed by rain, we race with sea
gulls inland, in faith like them
we will outfly the storm,
the tall grass bending
before us.

IN THE SANCTUARY[2]

Begin with the surface of things:
tarred road hedged by reeds,
wide flat ponds of the delta.
Flamingo posed in a pink arc,
the black scythe of its beak.
Flamingo
like a white stick flying,
the flames of its wings
snuffed by distance,
the air around it charred,
blackening.

Here, where earth and water
have often changed places,
the sky lowers its velvet mantle
on saltpans, cattle ranches,
the village a carnival
of postcards and kitsch.
White cars crowd the sea wall.
Above red roofs and bull ring
looms the church tower, massive
stone weight.

Ducking our heads
we enter darkness:
St Sarah's crypt, bones
in a glass box, robed
black idol, pilgrims
at her feet upon their knees.
And though I am not
one of these who light candles,
or offer her flowers, old
photographs, old griefs,
I can't help but be swayed
by the rhythms of prayer,
the pressure of bodies,
the threat out there
of flood and thunder,
to see as they have always seen
these flames in her eyes
and on her lips
this smile
beyond belief.

ACTS OF WORSHIP

The women in kerchiefs, long sleeves and flowered skirts,
frown at my sundress out of place in this place I can't leave
though you pull at my arm, complain of the heat, the air
ancient with incense, the must of burned candles.
What holds me here is what I can't read in capsule histories,
the weight in this temple underground, the worship of centuries.
The women whisper their prayers, inch on their knees
close to the stone they scratch for the dust
which powdered and watered may bless with fertility.
What matters how they address her: Matres, Artemis,
Isis, Cybele, Sarah-la-Kali, Saint of the gypsies.
Her names a chant in tongues that are used to silence,
her names invoke rituals of blood, commands of the womb
that contracts even now as my firstborn takes my hand,
leads me up out of the darkness under the earth
into this day's fury of wind, the sky split open. Hail rocks
the car as later you and I will rock, kneeling in the haven
of our tumbled bed, salt on the tongue, sacred salt,
salt of her primal sea.

VISITATION ON THE BEACH

The sea so salt, we barely have to move to stay afloat
adrift in the old dream: boat without oars or sail,
the boy's dream, waking in the pitch of summer night
translated to the advent of the saint on this bare shore,
a story we thought ours alone made myth, our reason
for visiting the temple and the town.

On the beach, an old woman lies in wait, breasts
on offer to the sun, her fingers tracing silver marks
that snake her belly and her thighs, proof of what
her body's done. Been and done. We skirt her nesting place,
avert our eyes from her too obvious flesh,
her stare so naked and her soft, impatient sighs

I mimic for a laugh and then catch breath, an itch like sand
grips my crotch, and in my mouth the sudden secret brine.

(STILL

    (months later,
riding the bus to work in the city,
head against the cool face of glass,
I peel back layers of clouds,
—so many shades of gray—
to the sun that is here so hot
it blinds colour: sea and sky and beach
the same blank slate. Sand burns
bare skin; air and water body
temperature
        (so that bundled as I am
    in my red coat, hands gloved
    in wool mittens, beside me
    only books and papers,
    eyes sting with grit
    that even without wind
    sifts along this shore
        (and you
      buried up to the neck in it, our son
      with his little shovel, laughing,
      as you rise naked and roaring,
      an eruption of the earth itself,
      chase him into water which parts
      and folds over you both, holding
      both of you in its salt embrace

                    (as I have also done,
              each in turn, root and seed,
              wrapped in my arms, your
              mouths on my breasts
                              (what
    spills over
onto these leafless woods, fallow
fields. The highway drifts
around a curve and there,
silver tarnished by cold breath,
the lake whose wrinkles blur
the darkening horizon. Again
that ringing in my ears, that
aching hum as if a song,
a hymn perhaps, rises
here unbidden, heart
in my own mouth.

IN SITES MADE SACRED

Hear the sea, restless, reflecting every nuance of gray
the sky can show it, paring available light in slivers,
silver on the tide's dark spell.

Spill of sunlight through a canopy of leaves,
the lush tangled musk of woods beckons us deeper, hushed,
hand in hand, away from the shore

the sure edge of waterline and dunes, the predictable
advances and retreats. Dwarfed by the green
archaic muddle we go back

beyond what we remember to a circle of sun, a stone table,
water cupped in a cracked hollow ringed by wildflowers,
blooms bowed.

We kneel to read the runes etched in lump and groove:
starred phallus, haloed womb, figures twined and twinned,
some dated last year,

some tens of centuries ago. Sensing us, a mantis raises
thin green arms in defiance, in prayer for mercy, in fear
of what looms over all of us

exposed here on the naked earth. Heat wavers over stone,
a shiver that translates these signs we touch into a breath:

breeze fingering bared neck, a quiver down the spine,
a whisper that beckons, that won't leave us yet alone.

CONFRONTING THE SOURCE[3]

We almost expect to see her crouched
in the bole of the flowering myrtle
that bisects the trail, that makes us duck
to pass beneath its branches: a black statue,
rough-hewn and round. It's that feeling
that follows us everywhere, catches the throat
when we drive past a menhir, a stone standing
in a flat field. Its eye open.

There's nothing here but bees. And the growing
rumble of water as we go down, the cliffs closing in.
It's farther than we thought, the way so steep
and slippery underfoot that I take your hand
and you lean back towards me. We're almost hugging
on the final slope, stumble out of forest tangle
to a clearing so deep in the gorge, the sun's
a faint reflection.

Out of a dark cleft in the limestone cliff,
at the crotch where the hills come together,
the river erupts, a gush of mist and thunder.
No wonder that we so quickly turn away
to the ruin of a mill, a thing a man made,
making use of the rush of white water.
As if walls and wheels could tame this outpouring.
As if, in spite of guidebooks and signposts,
we are not, in this of all places, trespassing.

UNDER THE SURFACE[4]

Going down into the mountain, we leave this June afternoon
to follow a torch through passages of bloodred stone
where water drips its mineral salts, grows columns, icicles,
cones. We need a name for them and for the story
the guide will tell us in a language only half
whose words we understand, our ears trip on accent,
idioms. We shuffle single file behind her, silent,
heads bowed under the weight of the rock piled over us,
feet slip on the worn, uneven path. We have read descriptions,
seen the postcards in the kiosk at the cavern mouth,
but what we come to in the hollow at the core—
la grotte des demoiselles, la cathédrale de pierre—
so wide and deep we can see neither floor nor ceiling,
the walls a tracery of gargoyle forms and faces—
stops us.
How long severed from the circle of the sun, the moon's
tidal pull, have we and those who have come before us
in her name stood here, crowded together against the dank
exhalations of the earth. One light spots the pillar
in the centre of the hall—*la Vierge*—the long fall
of fluted rock the hair that shawls the baby in her arms.
How long before someone, that mother who is tired
of carrying her fussing child, who has shushed
and threatened it the whole voyage through the dark,
resorts to song, lullaby or psalm. How long
before the first prayers come. Prayers
we forgot we remember swell in our throats,
give voice, gravel-tongued.

THE ORACLE SPEAKS

Dread the advent
        of the full moon
the nights
    (men always said)
belong to us

And she
they call her
    queen
    lover
    goddess   (though they invade her
                  with rockets
              spy on her
                  nakedness)
and she and
the sea
    conspire
against us
lure our men
        away from us (odysseys, they say
            are
                necessary)

She will yet turn
our men
      away from us
They will turn
      their eyes
      in distaste
away from us
         to her
         to the moon
         to metaphor

COMING OF AGE

THE MUMMY

In the museum it's the only thing he wants to see,
he frets through halls of armour, scarcely stopped
by thin curved blades of scimitars. Dinosaurs
he's seen so often before he can't be bothered
to do more than glance, ignores his favourite diorama
under sea, the gaping jaws of prehistoric fish, eerie
echoes of electronic sound. The mounted skins
of mammals and of birds disgust him most, he
can't believe that someone killed them all,
on purpose, an education just in this.

It's the dead woman who enthralls him, draws him
through room after room of pottery shards,
scale models of temples and tombs. Beyond
resurrection or rebirth, human clay laid out
by loving human hands, she lies here still.
Nose and palms pressed flat against her case,
kneeling, hushed, without question as close
as he can get, he considers how familiar
are the knobs and hollows of her face, compares
the length of fingers, counts her curled toes.

SON UNDERGROUND

i
He enters so willingly
the stone cold, the crack
in the limestone crust

ii
Lowering himself, feet first,
head bent, his hand on the rough lip
skeleton visible

iii
If I touch with one finger
the back of that hand: delicate tendons
crook into claws

iv
Neither waiting nor thinking of waiting,
he crawls the wet tongue of tunnel
crabwise

v
His penlight skitters on quartz seam,
fossil shells, glitter of ice chips,
winks, and is gone

vi
When even the earth is not solid
the echoes he raises
are easily swallowed

vii
He slips through the last gap: so light
this hand on my wrist
holding to, holding on

COUNTRY MATTERS

I've never seen such fields of corn and wheat, you tease,
as we drive down roads through farms so carefully plotted.
Such acres of sunflowers confused by clouds, heads
turned every which way and some given up, hung over,
wind shaking from them a long sigh. Our son's,
in the other room, in the dark of a farmhouse, shuttered,
on a night with no moon, the toss of his limbs
chafing starched sheets like these we have kicked
out of the way of our thrashing, stifling cries
we can't have him hear. He's too big now to sleep
in our bed, all of us nude in the heat, his cock
rises like yours in the morning, no joke, his face
at our door forlorn, eyes on his feet, rooted.
At the least we want, if the flower must bend
its bright head, that the sun be supplanted
not by the soft insistence of fog, but ravished
by thunder, fork lightning; breathtaken; stormed.

GONE FISHING

Out on the lake an hour after dawn, the moon's ghost
a white disc above hills humped under all that sky.
Our son stands upright in the bow, shifts to the swell
licked up by a wind cedars cradle in their long arms.
His body still but for the flick of wrist as he plays the rod,
lures whatever will take the bait, rise to the net I hold
for him to reel it in. Fish heaves the awful emptiness of air,
sucks the bare inch of wash in the bilge as you with delicate
touch remove the hook from its lip. Cupped in my hands,
this slippery tremor of scales, prick of fins, convulsive gasp
as I flip it over the gunwale, a splash that sends
the gulls hysteric. We kneel, eyes inches from the surface,
follow the shadow of his catch down to deeps known
only in the shiver of dreams. Only in dreams,
the surge of white wings tugs at our shoulders.
Only in dreams the symmetry of flight, over
and under the boat, the rings around us
widening.

SIEGE OF HERONS, MURDER OF CROWS[5]

Six herons in a line along a marshy shore
stiff-necked, intent not on the three of us
creeping down the path, but on whatever moves
under the surface. Still as sentries
in their patient hunger.

Or crows on the road's soft shoulders, hunched
like priests over entrails, greedy to find a living
in the dead. Murder and siege,

old stories we never have enough of, fables
that fascinate with dread. Our son
charges them, mimics their croaks
as they haul themselves into air
in a clamour of wings.

He stands their ground, fists on hips, head cocked
to watch them disappear. Then swallows hard
as if he too feels this itch: quills that prickle
down our spines.

COMING OF AGE

      1.
When you see what is wrong with your mother,
when you learn you are the one who will have to
take care of her, you begin collecting bottles
from their hiding places, under linens in the airing closet,
under the laundry sink, under nylon panties in her hamper.
The furnace gurgle chases you upstairs past the room
where she lies *having a little snooze* in the gold brocade
rocking chair: she snores, she snuffles turning over,
one hand against her cheek where you might want to press
your lips but you're afraid to wake her. You throw
the emptied bottles in the trash, free for this little while
though you know you can never find them all, the way
you never find your birthday presents no matter
how carefully you comb the corners of the house.
This is your coming of age, your trial: to wake in the night
alerted by the creeping in the hall, the creaking of the stairs,
the muffled curses when the empty cupboards slam.
Paper rustles, the awful clink of glass.
Clinking nightmare fingers of the man-without-a-head
who waits to swallow you as he's swallowed her.
You've seen it happen more than once and more
than in your dreams: he's trapped her in the cellar in the dark,
her head bent so far back, neck throbbing as she gulps,
is gulped, white knuckles on the gaping throat of glass.

2.

When your mother dies, you are twenty-one still
on your honeymoon learning what it is to be a man
living with a woman. For the first time since before
you can remember, you sleep naked in a woman's
naked arms, your lips on her full breast.

In the three days your mother passes
from coma to oblivion you can't make yourself
enter the IC room where her body lies
hooked to tubes, machines clucking over her.
Trauma is the purple mask of her face,
the brain scan's reluctant blips.

While you wait, you pace green halls, avoid
the stares of patients, interns. Outdoors
in the sun, gardeners bend over their plots,
preparing for harvest. All you can see
is that vegetable life, fruitless,
a future of rotting.

Your bride bolts upright from a dream,
her hand on her head where someone
strokes her hair, her mother-in-law
gone far beyond a joke. When the phone
shrills, you don't need to answer it.
You don't need anyone to tell you
your mother's better dead.

3.
You have kept the key to the front door of the house you grew up in and you open it into a silence that dries the welcome in your throat. Her favourite chair holds out its arms, a futile comfort.

Where do you begin to erase her life? With the curtains she hung, the furniture she so carefully arranged, the dishes she washed and left in the drainer. On the rim of a glass, you trace her lips' last crescent.

Your hand hovers over the newel post where she hit her head, which killed her. How could she fall? So many times she travelled up and down these stairs, in darkness and in light. Did she cry

when she saw him, the man-with-no-head come out of the cellar at last, his arms held out to catch her? You have to wonder in the end: did she choose to fly to him, her eyes and mouth wide open?

REUNION

It is all a question of semantics
you know: freedom, happiness.

She owns this house.
She drove me here from the station
in her car already paid for.
Her furniture is comfortably modern.
Her husband stays reading
in his own room at the top of the stairs.

Oh we discuss, you know, everything,
the years since our last meeting.
She is a teacher, she has two
grown children. We share
mutual friends, difficult mothers.

Around the careful pauses of our talk,
her Siamese stalks at the end of his leash.
The full moon tugs the night away from the lamp posts.
In the park, under flowering trees,
cats mate and howl.

WHEN FRIENDS DIVORCE

Easy to look at a marriage from the outside in,
the vanity of glass reflecting only what it wants to see

so to wake from this dream of the final fight between the two
of you, my jaws aching with the effort not to interfere.

Left in the dark, I'm not sure whose house I'm in, or when,
expect the light to turn on, Mom to enter, her finger on her lips.

These are the scents the sheets release as I turn over: cotton
dried on the line, flushed and flaking skin, salt, sweat.

Those pale squares are windows and the open bedroom door,
dense shadows the furniture I have so often dusted.

The furnace coughs, the loose pane rattles. Listen:
only my breath, my husband's rhythmic breath. Even in sleep

he generates such heat I can wrap it round us, in arms
for the day that has yet to come, its light pinched raw.

PARTING FRIENDS

     1.
Because of the intensity of colour: clear blue sky; yellow leaves
drifting against the high boards of a fence stained green
and tumbling in their lazy twist from black maple branches;
red brick of the house wall; cedar graying on the porch rail.

Because the smell of the smoke of the cigarettes
you keep lighting, puffing, grinding out
in a jam jar lid already full of ashes
recalls the plumes of fires that wafted
through neighbourhoods like this
when we were kids together, before
the city forbade such burning.

Because the dog snuffling for her ball kicks up the leaves,
a rustle releasing the sweet dry odour of decay
that children triumph over in their charge
through curbside piles on their way to school.
Because she drops it at your feet and you ignore it
as you ignore her frantic tail, her wide mouth
all tongue and teeth.

Because you are crying.

Because you are trying not to cry. Because you are the one
who has left the family home. You are the one who has said
there's still life waiting.

2.
What I want to hear about
is the villain,
the snake in the grass,
who at least
tempted one of you
with sweet
forked tongue:
a parable

you'll have no part of.
Pacing the garden
raked and mulched
for winter, you point
out facts: apples
on the neglected tree
grow stunted
fall still yellow,
skin unblemished
rotten at the core

blighted fruit, fit
only for the compost.

And though I say
there's heat in there, a slow
still sure combustion,
you're through
with such chemistry.
Breathing fire, you
poke holes in all
my neat constructions,
scar the fence rail
that divides us
with your burning
butts.

3.

The child knows who to blame: wicked
mother, tyrant father, her own evil
alien self.

Days she shuffles from house to house
it's always pouring, her coat too thin,
umbrella missing. Her wet face
lowered, she won't look up
to see you waiting for her
at the open door

and none of you can say
which bed's the coldest:
the one you bend to straighten
when she's gone, fall
into its small hollows
her teddy in your arms

or the one you lie on
beside her, her head
under the pillow,
back rigid, clinging
to the mattress edge,
sheets of ice between you.

THIN ICE

All of us play at reconciliation,
a game of shinny on the backyard rink,
where bluelines shadow thin ice:

you and me and your daughter
against our husbands and my son.
Last year, it was family vs family

when you were still a family. (Now
it's two on one, power plays, goals
missed and disputed.)

Thwack of stick on stick, the shush of skates:
your husband crouched, ready to glove
any shot you try to get by him.

The kids have given up, cold feet, fed up
with the fights, you at one end, he
at the other, the two of us

circling between you, unwilling
to be audience or referees.
You've also had enough,

but he isn't ready to quit. The surface
chips under our blades, brings us
to our knees. Call it a draw

if you want. Or a victory. Whatever
it's time to be done with this, admit
that it's over.

THE DAUGHTER ELEMENT

1.
She, sitting on a rock at the water's edge,
allows her hair to curtain her eyes as she dispels
with a taut smile and negligent wave of her hands
the story she has brought me here to tell. Ducks
home in on us, alert to the flick of her wrist
as she picks buttercups apart and flings
petals in the current. Their learned response
to the hand's motion: come, food. Mates
for life. Loves, loves not. Like
throwing bread upon the waters.

Like sin that is never original, follows
the same old path, though the first time
you come to hear of it, it takes
your breath away. Heir to the flesh,
decay eats at her, forms a lump
beneath her heart. What the father
has done cannot be undone
and there is no health in her.
Friend my own age she is still
that dead man's forsaken daughter.
This is why she is starving,
why she is always so hungry.
If I tried to hug her now
she would break, her hold
that brittle.

2.
Too hot to care about coliform counts,
we hike upriver from the public beach
to a pool carved into the bank
stilling the current. Here
we immerse ourselves wholly
in clear water, dive again and again
and never touch bottom. At last
we lay ourselves down
where limestone shelves
make warm shallows. Light
flickers in ripples, a lens
that, wavering, magnifies
fossil leaves and fishes.
I can trace them if I want.
My huge pale fingers
fumble into braille.

The signs she looks for: dreams
she annoys me with, their symbols
hieroglyphic, that wake her
even from a doze: four horses
come down to the other shore,
eyes wide, foam in their teeth,
flanks still heaving.
To be given such an image.

To share it. She touches
my hand, finger to her lips.
I blink and the white foal
shakes its head, casts
diamonds of light
and water she grips
in both fists, wrings
from them
what she can
of joy.

3.
It's how I'm moved always
to turn landscape into literature,
my knapsack carefully packed
with maps, bird books, guides
to flowers, rocks, trees. The names
down pat. As for her story,
I can give her fictions
that promise to be true, case
studies, biographies: myths
that prove that all of this
has happened in another life,
before. That nothing's new.
We've reached the same point
on the river and it's different,
the ducks gone, the water
sullen brown. She cups
the current in her hand,
pours water palm to palm.
Things shift,
catch us unawares,
the surface a long tremor
that knocks us
into each other.
In the shock after
I am left wordless
and all she is
is light.

4.
Sometimes, it is not a matter of the body only,
but the way that it moves into and through landscape,
how muscle and nerve work to keep it level
in its juggle with gravity, the kick of speed,
the thrill of falls we rise from flushed, breathless,
hearts pumping, aware of the vast indifference
of the earth to our impact. To be blinded
in the moment of passing by the particular light
the season throws on the river and its reflections.
To return to the rapids up the wide trail from the lake
or chance cutting cross country, follow pink ribbons
tied to black trunks. *Do you know where you are?*
asks one sign after another and we do in one sense,
we've been here before when the leaves were green
and the wind mimicked water in their rustling.
Now, without speaking, we stop, rest on our poles,
faces tilted to the sun, its warm hands on our cheeks.
Eyes closed; intent; listening. The rub
of bare limbs. Their rhythmic whisper.
Even under ice, the current seethes.
We are caught by that rush. For a time
frozen. Still. In this place
together.

VIRGIN TERRITORY

FIRST TIME

So far
back in the woods:
shush
of skies,
grind
of bindings

So far back
without a map,
I can imagine:
we are
first come
here
      (ignore
the signs:
the tracks
we follow)

And later still
breath raw,
past the ache
   of needing
   to explore,
shivering
we fall back
in drifts of
snowy sheets,

too late
for caution:
hush
no words
for now

not the first time
we've been here
                    before

VIRGIN TERRITORY . . .

there is none, we know that, the whole earth
has been measured and plotted, its species,
even the dying ones, numbered. Science
goes by camera undersea to lost continents;
maps the skies; sends satellites to probe
secrets of the planets, their rings, their
many moons. Beyond the known radius
of our sun, telescopes track the swirl
of galaxies, fix on nebulae, mark
black holes.

Everything once mysterious sucked in,
tales of gods and heroes dead stars
we know only in their passing. Still
we can't help it, we are drawn
from the stripped bed out to the garden
where sheets hang limp on a white line.
A sudden breeze a breath that lifts long hair
that lifts and drops these linens
the way we have done, under them,
making them billow, our heads turned away,
unable to face eyes all pupil

as now, in the hour of eclipse, we can't look
as sun and moon come together. If this
should visit us only once in our generation,
let us stand up for it, let us lower our eyes
and close our busy mouths, our hands
clasped as the shadow falls over us.
Even the birds have fallen silent, wait
for the light we have taken so for granted
to be divided from the darkness
as it was in the beginning. See:
the halo throbs.

EVENSONG[6]

Lie with me on the red quilt in the dew of August,
the sky above us streaked with meteors, so many stars
we give up naming them

give up the telling of stories, the ones
handed down to us, the ones we make
to people the lonely dark.

A log in the stone ring crumbles to embers, water
laps among reeds, tall grass cradles us,
the scent of its dying incenses

the fear that would bring us to our knees.
Salvation begins with the love of bodies
coming together,

the only time since the womb let go of us
our hearts beat with the blood of another
pulse in a perfect fit.

Put your left hand under my head, with your right hand
embrace me. When I found you, the one I love,
I held you, I will not now let you go.

MOUTH TO MOUTH

When you fall off the dock we are laughing,
it's been one of those weekends: rain
and the hot water heater blowing its fuses.

Between storms, we come down
to look at the moon, high and haloed,
the lake so still there is almost silence:
no crickets, no mosquitoes, no loons.

You step back, become a clown,
open-mouthed, arms embrace air.
The long second before the splash.
The longest second comes
before your gasp and curse.

Hands on heart and mouth to mouth
we play charades: both of us sacrifice
and saving grace.

SPEAKING IN TONGUES

We've walked along this trail before
but only in midsummer. Now, from its height,
the lake seen through stripped tree branches
appears a gleaming slit between two hills
tufted with conifers, the granite cliffs
at the narrows knees raised and spread.
Waves rock under a fingering wind, sun
strokes whitecaps to a lather we recognize,
licking our lips. So we lay ourselves down
on a bed of dry moss, help ease off
each other's heavy clothes. This
is where we arrive at last and again,
in a tangle of tongues and limbs,
hands claws rooting to hold on,
to urge desire, want and need
the same clenched thrust, the words
spilling out of our mouths
yes, oh

UTTER SILENCE

In this moment after we finish making love, after the echo
of our cries has faded, and our blood relaxes in a rhythm
we are so used to we don't hear it drumming any more.
In this one moment before limbs assert themselves,
shrug off a heavy leg, an arm; before skins shrink
from the damp press of sweat; before the musk of sex
wrinkles noses, foreheads: listen.
We are too much involved in the world's constant palaver,
we bicker, we discuss, even our private dreams
are told in stories, symbols we can find in books,
the clamour of signs demands our attention.
Only in this moment can we renounce with full hearts
the treasure of speech for the pleasure of flesh,
this flesh we cling to such a little while. Listen,
when we are still one with and in our bodies,
the silence consumes us, leaves us
for a moment so close, so utterly
abandoned.

THE LURE OF THE DEEP

       1.
Drawn, in spite of timetables and weather,
to go down, once again, to the ocean shore,
we scurry barefoot up over the last hump of dunes,
gravity forcing us to our knees before we can face
that vast heave, the horizon. We button jackets,
thrust hands deep in pockets, bow heads as wind
brings tears to our eyes, turns us away
from whatever clouds do to light on water.
Three-clawed runes lead us to the edge,
the Atlantic frothing in its final exhaustion
licks our toes, lays before us shells, pebbles,
glittering green wrack. We walk
past families, stray tourists, their dogs,
till the beach is ours alone. But there,
out there, in a trough between swells,
a woman, waist deep, back turned to us,
hair shawling her shoulders, hand to eyes,
stares out to sea.

2.
When you make friends with a man,
you learn navigation, how to steer
narrow channels, avoid undertows,
cross currents. When you meet him,
you brush cheeks, right and left,
lips kissing air, the tingle of skin
not quite touching. When you walk
together on the beach, fully clothed,
arms swinging, husband and wife
walk with you, their hips insistent
press against you, their hands
a welcome weight around your waists.
Children run between you
and the sea's enticing lap.
Little arms flapping, they
plunge into a flock of gulls,
a mass of swirling white,
a raucous choir.

3.
The swimmer arches her body, leaps
into surf, a tug I feel in my spine, roots
of wings, dormant fins, hair that lifts
on the back of the neck. She surfaces
far out beyond the breaking crests, raises
an arm to wave to someone I can't see
waiting for her in the dunes. Or to us.
Calling her siren can't explain the lure
of the deep, her distance, how she
would hook us with words, reel us in
with stories. We sigh, turn our backs
on the sea, trudge to the car park.
Light breaks through clouds
in flames we flee from inland
and her song that would scorch us,
burns in us.

CELEBRATING THE SOLSTICE[7]

Out of the wilderness of wooded granite hills that press in
on the lake, a tear of blue in the undulating green canopy—
a voice cries out and we can't tell at first if it's bird or human
or merely once human. Ghosts belong to the long evenings
of early summer when the light is a gray curtain between
what we can see and what we only imagine, the stars coming out
one by one by one until suddenly the dome of sky reels
with them, so many of them the stories they've been given
cannot be deciphered. In the city the feast of St John
is a parade tall buildings attempt to belittle, to muffle
with busy windows the stamping of feet in unison,
the raising of flags, the slogans chanted in a language
universal as the hot rattle of a gun aimed
at a roomful of the chosen before it turns on itself.
In the past we have picnicked halfway up the mountain,
above us the shining crypt where the saint's heart beats
in its red chalice. Another myth for the dark. Today
we foraged for deadfall, bare and needled branches, cones
which now burn blue in a circle of stones, drawing us closer.
The damp seeps in from the lake's edge with the hoarse
songs of frogs, rustling in the bush resurrects fears of men
who rage over the loss of their land for farms and golf courses,
fears we pretend to banish with the toasting of marshmallows,

spun sugar flaming on the tips of sharpened sticks. Mosquitoes
and black flies rise with the night, our mouths not full enough
of words or music to keep their whining out. Slapping
our own flesh, we desert the fire for the haven of the tent,
trusting its thin walls to repel the ravenous attack, unsure
whether to praise or curse ourselves for running away
to the wilds of second-growth forest. We abandon the stars
to the insidious creeping clouds, the streets to whooping revels
that want no part of us. The earth is a hard bed; dreams
forsake even this, the shortest night. We lie still
in our separate bags, mummied in down, listen
to the patter of rain, the loon's anxious wail.
We are too old for this. All our bones are on fire.

ACTS OF COMMUNION[8]

> *"What is your beloved*
> *more than another beloved*
> *that you should so charge us?"*
> —the Song of Solomon

1.
Let him kiss me with the kisses of his mouth,
this my beloved and my friend. Let me
for the space of one evening close the books,
turn off the radio and TV. It is not that I do not
acknowledge the sins and wickedness the world
lays bare for me, not that I dare to pretend
I am less than alone, nor guiltless. I cannot walk
by myself under the flowering trees in the park,
the repairman who comes to my house rubs past me
saying sorry, licking his teeth, pliers open in his fist.
The lilies wilt, their leaves turn yellow in the rain.
Even though butterflies are born without wings—
for three hours, four, let me forget this, let me
look on love and hear the voice of his desire.

2.
In the back seat of the taxi and in the restaurant
until the waiter leaves us, we say nothing,
we touch comfortably and in passing.
The clatter of forks and knives,
the chatter of other conversations
whirl their cocoon of noise around us.
Wine is poured, bread steams in its basket.
What goes on beneath the linen cloth
where trousered leg presses stockinged knee:
discourse of skin, subtext of ardent bone.
We do not need to stir up or awaken love
until it pleases: our lips unfurl
and the wine goes down smoothly.

3.
Choir of wrens in a trellis of vines.
Table, basket of bread, white plate,
rounds of melted cheese.
Spilled wine bleeds on the cloth.
Your hand on the cloth
striped by sunlight. Fine hair
black on your forearms, black
in the open neck of your shirt.
Scar on your throat
throbs as pulse slows,
breath evens.
We sit back, my palm
held open out to you
offering, this close
we've come to grace:
take, eat.

A KIND OF CATECHISM

                    Without the moon the sky
a sieve of starlight. Without a breeze the lake
a silver plate cupped in the hills' dark hands.
What has brought us down through the tunnel of trees
where nothing scurries or buzzes or squeaks
but holds its breath, on tiptoe, eyes unblinking?
What has taught us that words will only sully
the dispensation wine has blessed us with
to strip and lower ourselves without ripple or gasp
naked over the dock into water warmer than the air?
What draws us out from the shadows of the shore,
fingers and feet move barely enough to stay afloat
flat on our backs, arms spread to embrace the aurora
that shimmers and flares from the northern horizon,
thrilling the universe with a green and rosy pulse
that moves us also beyond the touch of a lover's hand,
your hand coaxing my lips to open, my arms and legs
hugging you, holding you in, pulling you under
with me anointed by this flood that loosens our tongues
into vowels of praise, avowals of naming. Who are we
to honour in this way? Who are we
to be so honoured?

ENDNOTES

1. BIRDS OF PASSAGE
". . . the *langue des oiseaux* [the language of the troubadours, the poets of Languedoc] . . . is rich in multilingual puns, double-entendre, allusions both classical and biblical, paradox and allegory. In this language of *gay saber*, playful and tricksterish, nothing can be taken at face value."
—Ean Begg, *The Cult of the Black Virgin*. Penguin/Arkana, 1985. pp. 137-8.

2. IN THE SANCTUARY
After the crucifixion, three Marys—the mother of apostles James and John, the sister of the Virgin, and Mary Magdalene—were put to sea in a boat without oars or sails. Their black Egyptian servant, Sarah, wept so piteously to join them that they threw a cloak on the waters on which she walked out to the boat. They landed in the Camargue at the mouth of the river Rhône at Ratis, the site of a Roman temple whose name refers to Ra, who piloted the boat without oars or sails in the Egyptian Book of the Dead. Isis, Artemis, and Cybele were worshipped on this spot which had previously been a place of worship of the Celtic triple goddess Matres.
The bones of St Sarah are in the church's crypt. She is the patron saint of the gypsies, who call her Sarah-la-Kali, connecting her to the Hindu god. In the crypt along with the black statue of the saint, is a Mithraic relief of a bull-slaying, from the dust of which fertility potions have been made.
—paraphrased from the *Cadogan Guide to the South of France*, by Dana Facaros and Michael Pauls. London: Cadogan Books, 1992.

3. CONFRONTING THE SOURCE
The source of the river Vis is reached after a long hiking descent of the gorge in the Cirque de Navacelles: "A *cirque* looks like a deep lunar crater though it is in fact a loop dug deep into the limestone . . . by the meandering river Vis long ago."
—from *The Cadogan Guide to the South of France*.

4. UNDER THE SURFACE
Grotte des Demoiselles near the village of St-Bauzille-de-Putois in the Cévennes highlands, is "a cave discovered in 1889 that has one of France's most spectacular displays of pipe-organ stalactites and stalagmites" (from *The Cadogan Guide to the South of France*). The stalagmite in the central cave looks something like a woman holding a baby: a madonna, in fact. Catholic masses are held here on the Feast of the Assumption and at Christmas.

5. SIEGE OF HERONS, MURDER OF CROWS
These phrases are generic terms for flocks of these birds in the way one would say "pride of lions" or "litter of pups".
—William Packard, *The Poet's Dictionary*. Harper/Perennial, 1989.

6. EVENSONG
The Cathars believed in part that "Salvation begins with the love of bodies" and that orgasm represented the perfect fit between flesh and spirit (see Ean Begg, *The Cult of the Black Virgin*).
The final stanza is paraphrased from the *Song of Solomon* in the New King James Version of the Bible.

7. CELEBRATING THE SOLSTICE
" . . . in the worship of St John [the Baptist, June 24] the people made three manners of fire: one was of clean bones and no wood and that is called a bone fire; another of clean wood and no bones and that is called a wood fire . . . and the third is made of wood and bones and that is called St John's fire."
—from the *Festyvall of 1493*, quoted in *Brewer's Precise Dictionary of Phrase & Fable*. Oxford: Helicon, 1993.

8. ACTS OF COMMUNION
Several lines in this poem are taken from the *Song of Solomon* (NKJV).